AF668820

Ex Libris

Name ____________________

Address ____________________

____

Telephone ____________________

Fax ____________________

e-mail ____________________

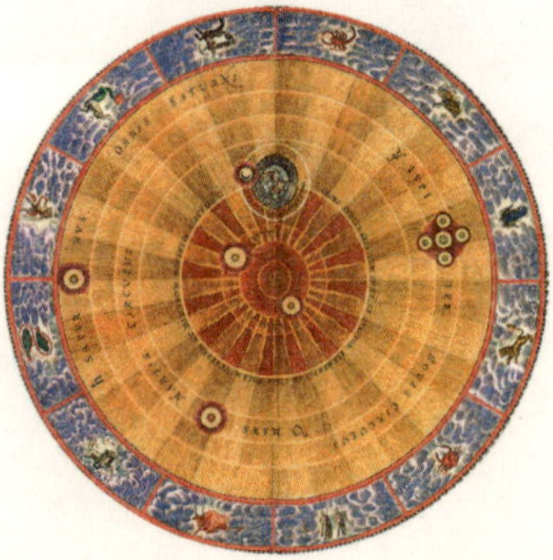

Text

Natalidita Ningthoukhongjam

© Kalabindu Enterprises P. Ltd.

ISBN: 978-93-5036-850-3

Cover image: Kenny Tong/Shutterstock.com

Astronomer's monument at the Griffith Observatory in Los Angeles, California

OFFSHOOT

Kalabindu Enterprises P. Ltd.

GF–18, Virat Bhawan

Commercial Complex, Mukherjee Nagar

Delhi 110009

Phone: +91-11-47038000

Beyond IMAGINATION

PERSECUTED FOR THEIR IDEAS

A NOTEBOOK

Introduction

The great Irish playwright George Bernard Shaw once said: “Progress is impossible without change and those who cannot change their minds cannot change anything.” And rightly said, for the world we know today, with its technological wonders and vast pool of knowledge, could not have reached such a high state of development had it not been for the people who dared to think different. When we trace the evolution of humankind, we see how human beings moved from one level to the next—from hunting and gathering food to farming to founding whole civilizations to developing computers and smartphones. If the first person to discover fire had shrunk away from it in terror, wouldn’t it have taken us longer to become who or what we are today?

Yet change itself is a source of fear to many. This may be because we are comfortable with the systems we have grown up believing in, or because changing the norms compromise those in power. Whatever the reason, men and women capable of posing such a threat have suffered throughout history. While some suffered ridicule and exile, others were imprisoned, even executed.

In this notebook we will read about thirteen scientists and thinkers who helped shape the modern world but suffered discrimination and opposition in their lifetime. There are familiar names such as Copernicus and Galileo. A few such as Rhazes and Averroes are less heard of. The common thread binding all of them is the exceptional talent they possessed and the courage that drove them despite all odds.

It is never easy to be different, to offer an alternate reality closer to the truth, but it is a task that must be fulfilled for the benefit and progress of humankind. And it is this task that Nature—or shall we say that inscrutable force which drives the universe—entrusted these luminaries with.

The School of Athens, Raphael, 1509–1511

Rhazes

(c.854–925)

Muhammad ibn Zakariya al-Razi or Rhazes lived more than a thousand years ago in Persia. He was a polymath[1] who excelled in many fields, including medicine, philosophy and chemistry. An avid writer as well as reader, he acquainted the Arabic world with Galen and Hippocrates, setting off a merging of two different approaches to medicine. In the words of British historian Edward Granville Browne, he was "probably the greatest and most original of all the physicians."

Rhazes was the first to distinguish between small pox and measles. He revolutionized the pharmacy methods of his time, innovating equipment such as flasks, spatulas and phials. He even argued that medical practice must be governed by ethics, targeting fake doctors as well as overconfident physicians. His translated works became a rage in Europe and at least two volumes of *Al Mansuri—'On Surgery'* and *A General Book on Therapy*—were incorporated into the medical curriculum of Western Universities. He eventually earned the sobriquet of 'Father of Pediatrics' because of his book *The Diseases of Children*, which established pediatrics as a separate medical field.

Although Rhazes worked as a successful doctor for most of his life, his outspokenness, rationalism and open criticism of traditional medical practices landed him in trouble. He was allegedly beaten with a manuscript of his own work as per the orders of a religious cleric. He went blind as a result of the assault.

In modern Iran, two institutes named after him have been set up to mark his special position in Persian history: Razi Institute in Tehran and Razi University in Kermanshah. August 27 is also celebrated as 'Razi Day' in his home country.

1. polymath: someone who knows a lot about different subjects

"The doctor's aim is to do good, even to our enemies."

— Rhazes

Averroes

(1126–1198)

Born in Córdoba (Spain), Averroes or Abūl-Walīd Muhammad Ibnh Ahmad Ibn Rušd is hailed as the father of secular thought in Western Europe. He enjoyed a productive life, working as a legal administrator and studying a wide range of subjects, ranging from classical music, geography and mathematics to astronomy, physics and medicine. The physical state of inertia was first correctly described by him.

Although Averroes was an influential polymath like Rhazes, the greatest impact he left was on the field of philosophy. Historians regard him as the man single-handedly responsible for reviving interest in Aristotelian philosophy. His commentaries on Plato and Aristotle earned him the popular title 'the Commentator,' and his writings were translated into Hebrew and Latin.

Interestingly, the same aspect of his learning that brought him so much fame would result in criticism and persecution. Impressed by Averroes's research on Greek philosophers, the caliph of Marrakesh (Morocco), Abu Yaqub Yusuf, appointed him as both chief judge and chief physician. However, the strict rationalism of Averroes, as well as his liberal interpretation of religion, earned him the ire of the religious community. This, along with Averroes's recognition of other kings and divinities in his writings, cost him his patron's favor. It is well documented that the jealousy of his peers, who vied with him for patronage, had a hand in his fall from grace with his patron. He was declared a heretic and exiled and his books were burnt.

If it hadn't been for Averroes, perhaps modern Western philosophy would have taken a longer time to evolve into what it is today. He was included in Dante's *Divine Comedy*, in which he appears in the 'place that favor owes to fame.' Famous writer Salman Rushdie claims in his memoir that his surname came from Averroes's original name 'Ibn Rushd.' Since 1999 the Ibn Rushd Prize for Freedom of Thought has been annually given to those promoting freedom of speech in the Arab world.

"The world is divided into men who have wit and no religion and men who have religion and no wit."

— Averroes

Nicolaus Copernicus

(1473–1543)

There was a time in the history of humankind when it was believed that the Earth was the center of the universe and that the Sun and other heavenly bodies revolved around it. This model was popularized by the Roman astronomer and mathematician Claudius Ptolemy around 150 CE. Although Aristarchus of Samos, an ancient Greek astronomer and mathematician, put forward the heliocentric model[1] as early as the third century BCE, it would not be until Nicolaus Copernicus presented his model of the universe that the geocentric theory[2] would meet with a serious challenger.

Born on February 19, 1473, in the city of Thorn, Poland, Copernicus was a thinker, mathematician, astronomer, economist and diplomat. He spoke five languages—Latin, German, Polish, Greek and Italian—and studied an array of disciplines, which included astrology, canon law and medicine. A versatile man blessed with keen observation and unwavering dedication, it wasn't long before he began to notice that Ptolemy's model of the universe could not account for certain alignments and movements of the heavenly bodies.

He wrote about his theory in his manuscript titled *On the Revolutions of the Celestial Spheres*, publishing it just before his death in 1543. Although he had his supporters, severe criticism rose from religious quarters. Even when he was alive, the Teutonic Order would hire clowns to make fun of him, calling him a 'crazy priest.' The Church finally put the book on the forbidden list in 1650, a ban that would be lifted only in 1822.

Today we remember him as the man who started a revolution in the field of astronomy. The chemical element 'Copernicium' was named after him in 2009. In their dedication, the discovery team called him "an outstanding scientist, who changed our view of the world."

1. heliocentric model: a cosmological model which states that the Sun is at the center of the solar system
2. geocentric theory: a theory which states that the Earth is at the center and the Sun revolves around it

"To know that we know what we know and to know that we do not know what we do not know, that is true knowledge."

— Nicolaus Copernicus

Giordano Bruno

(1548–1600)

It takes a certain amount of courage—even recklessness—to continuously oppose authority for the sake of one's belief in the truth. Giordano Bruno was one such man who exhibited this doggedness. He was born in 1548 in Nola, near Naples, as Filippo Bruno, and became an ordained priest of the Dominican Order at the age of twenty-four. Highly educated and the favorite of powerful patrons, he could have enjoyed an easy life. But being a free and fearless thinker, Bruno chose to follow his own path, even if it crossed the paths of others.

Bruno made contributions to several disciplines. He was well known for his extensive study on the art of memory. He also dabbled in mathematics and language. But his religious ideas were considered heretical and he had to flee Naples to avoid the Inquisitors. More problematic than this defiance of religious dogma, although more important for the evolution of science, were his basic concepts of cosmology.

If Copernicus proposed that the Earth moved around the Sun, then Bruno took that theory several steps further by claiming that the Sun was not the center of the universe—there were multiple worlds in space which could have life of their own. This controversial notion was one of the biggest reasons why he lost the protection of his patrons and became a prey of the Inquisition[1]. He was arrested in Venice in 1591 and tried, and retried in Rome in 1592, suffering interrogation for seven more years. Upon his refusal to give up his beliefs, he was burnt at the stake.

Though persecuted in his lifetime, Bruno would be exalted in the nineteenth and twentieh centuries as a martyr of science. He has featured in several fictional works, such as *Finnegans Wake* by James Joyce and *The Last Confession* by Morris West. A crater on the Moon and two asteroids have been named after him and the SETI (Search for Extra Terrestrial Intelligence) League presents the Giordano Bruno Memorial Award in his memory every year.

1. Inquisition: the judicial institution set up by the Roman Catholic Church to try people opposed to its beliefs

"Perhaps you pronounce this sentence against me with greater fear than I receive it."

— Giordano Bruno

Galileo Galilei

(1564–1642)

Galileo Galilei of Pisa was an inquisitive and innovative child. From an early age, he nurtured a habit of seeking out the truth. His father—Vincenzo Galilei, the celebrated lute player and music composer encouraged his son and persuaded him to study medicine at the University of Pisa, instead of pursuing priesthood. In the end Galileo had achieved much more than his father could have imagined—he became a physicist, mathematician, engineer, astronomer and philosopher.

Galileo played a major role in shaping modern physics and astronomy. His work with the simple pendulum, the telescope, the analysis of the parabola, as well as his discoveries in astronomy—the four largest moons of Jupiter, the difference between the appearance of the planets and the stars, and the presence of sunspots—were significant contributions. *Two New Sciences*, which was written in the later years of his life, established the two modern sciences, kinematics[1] and strength of materials.

Galileo supported the Copernican model of the universe; predictably, he too faced punishment for his bold theories. In 1633, in the same rooms where Giordano Bruno was interrogated by the Roman Inquisition, he was brought in to answer for his cosmological studies. He withdrew his claims finally but was put under house arrest for the rest of his life. His work *Dialogue Concerning the Two Chief World Systems, Ptolemic and Copernican* was put in the Catholic Church's Index of Forbidden Books, and would be removed only in 1835.

Tragic though his end was, Galileo Galilei would be appreciated for his efforts in the future, with great scientists like Stephen Hawking and Albert Einstein crediting him for the birth of modern science. The four largest moons of Jupiter are named 'Galilean moons' after him. His life is celebrated in songs such as *Bohemian Rhapsody* by Queen, and works of fiction such as *Life of Galileo* by Bertolt Brecht and *Lamp at Midnight* by Barrie Stavis.

1. kinematics: the study of the motion of bodies without considering the cause or effect of the motion

"And yet it moves."

— Galileo Galilei

Charles Darwin

(1809–1882)

Today we learn from our biology textbooks that humankind underwent a long process of evolution to reach our present state of being. But we did not always enjoy the benefits of such knowledge, nor did we have the luxury of studying about it freely at school. When Charles Darwin published his theory of evolution in his 1859 book, *On the Origin of Species,* most of the Western world believed in the Biblical concept of the birth of man. Once the scientific world was forced to sit up and notice his vision of how natural selection and survival of the fittest shaped us, there was no turning back.

Darwin's theory of natural selection, that states that living organisms evolve through a series of natural changes in traits as per their interaction with their environment, proved to be extremely unpopular. It removed the presence of a higher power guiding the design of humans. In short, it challenged the existence of God and that did not sit well with the religious sentiments of the time. People of the time were hardly willing to believe that humankind descended from apes. He faced harsh criticism from religious authorities and fellow scientists. Caricatures of Darwin as an orangutan were printed in newspapers. A heated public debate took place in Oxford in 1860, in which Darwin's supporters defended him against Samuel Wilberforce, the Bishop of Oxford.

In spite of the backlash, Darwin's studies and findings managed to convince most scientists in his lifetime. He was regarded as one who had presented, and defended with ample proof, revolutionary ideas. Darwin was buried at Westminster Abbey in honor of his path-breaking work. His name has been given to more than 120 species and nine genera, as well as a postgraduate college at Cambridge University.

"Light will be thrown on the origin of man."

— Charles Darwin

Gregor Mendel

(1822–1884)

For centuries crossbreeding had been practised by humans to produce plant and animal breeds that would possess desirable traits. How the process of crossbreeding itself determined the inheritance of traits was, however, not clearly or correctly known. Gregor Mendel, an Augustinian friar born in the then Austrian Empire, threw light on the subject by experimenting extensively with over 30,000 pea plants between 1856 and 1863. His findings were published in *Proceedings of the Natural History Society of Brünn* in 1866. The 'factors' that he found responsible for producing visible, predictable traits in the offspring, are now known as 'genes.'

However, the scientific community at large ignored Mendel's work. Firstly, the paper in which his work was published had limited circulation, so very few people knew about it. Secondly, his use of statistics and mathematics was too advanced and it confused the biologists of the time. Natural science in his era was mainly descriptive and confined to the classification of species. Thirdly, he suffered setbacks because he did not have the technological means to show physical evidence of the 'factors.' Finally, the scientific world was preoccupied with Darwin's revolutionary work on evolution and Mendel's relatively obscure research could not generate much interest.

During Mendel's lifetime, his discoveries were accepted only in relation to hybridization, not inheritance. In the early twentieth century, the same observations regarding inheritance of traits were made and verified by independent scientists—not only in plants but in humans and animals as well—resulting in renewed interest in his findings. These rules of heredity have therefore been named 'Mendelian inheritance.' Although overlooked in life, Mendel gained considerable posthumous fame and credit. He is now referred to as the 'Father of Genetics.'

"My scientific labors have afforded me great gratification and I am convinced that it will not be long before the whole world acknowledges the results of my work."

— Gregor Mendel

Ludwig Boltzmann

(1844–1906)

Much of the scientific knowledge that we readily accept as facts today took years to formulate; some even required sacrifices on the parts of those who discovered them. For Ludwig Eduard Boltzmann, celebrated Austrian physicist, teacher and philosopher, the effort to defend his theories would take a toll on his mental health. What were these theories that proved so controversial? One was the statistical mechanics theory of the branch of science that explains how atomic properties such as mass, charge and structure influence the physical properties of matter.

Ludwig Boltzmann's life was characterized by a seesaw of acceptance and opposition. As a lecturer of natural philosophy, he was highly popular. He was a prominent figure in the world of academics, becoming a member of the Imperial Austrian Academy of Sciences in 1885, the President of the University of Graz in 1887 and an elect member of the Royal Swedish Academy of Sciences in 1888. These achievements, however, would not protect him from conflict with other major scientists, such as Ernst Mach. Boltzmann started working on statistical mechanics as early as the 1870s and compiled his theories in *Lectures on Gas Theory* (1896). The application of statistics in Boltzmann's logic was not accepted by contemporary physicists. After years of fighting for his theories and facing repeated and fresh objections that threatened to rubbish his work, Boltzmann tragically committed suicide in 1906.

With the passage of time, Boltzmann's concepts were verified by several scientists. His name has been given to a wide variety of scientific ideas, such as Boltzmann brain, Boltzmann machine, Boltzmann factor, Boltzmann constant and Boltzmann distribution. In his honor the Commission on Statistical Physics of the International Union of Pure and Applied Physics (IUPAP) awards the Boltzmann Medal (or Boltzmann Award) once every three years to physicists who use statistical mechanics to acquire new scientific results.

"The most ordinary things are to philosophy a source of insoluble puzzles."

— Ludwig Boltzmann

Jagadish Chandra Bose

(1858–1937)

Indian polymath and science fiction writer, Sir Jagadish Chandra Bose, was a genius rarity in many ways. As an Indian who lived in the era of the freedom movement, when Indians in general were snubbed by the British, his determination helped him become a pioneer of science. He expanded the field of radio and microwave optics and is now commonly considered to be the father of wireless technology, as well as the first person to discover milliliter-length electromagnetic waves. He also invented the crescograph, an instrument that could record how plants responded to various external stimuli. Many of his still functional devices are kept on display at the museum at Bose Institute, Kolkata.

As illustrious as his body of work is, Bose faced a lot of obstacles on account of his race. At Presidency College, Calcutta, where he was a professor, he didn't receive proper funding for his research and he was paid much less in comparison to his British colleagues. Instead of throwing in the towel, Bose turned a small space next to a bathroom into a laboratory and carried on his research there. Due to lack of funds he would even buy the equipment he needed with his own money. He maintained that his innovations were purely for the advancement of science and so abstained from pursuing commercial and intellectual copyrights. Until recently, therefore, the scientific community at large credited Marconi for the invention of wireless technology.

Bose was recognized for his work during his lifetime. He became a Knight Bachelor in 1917 and was inducted into the Royal Society of London in 1920. In addition to that, he was a member of numerous other scientific academies and a founding fellow of the Indian National Science Academy. However, the racial prejudice he suffered for being Indian and dark-skinned deprived him of the true extent of the appreciation he deserved. The credit given to him has mostly been given in retrospect.

"The true laboratory is the mind, where behind illusions we uncover the laws of truth."

— Jagadish Chandra Bose

Lise Meitner

(1878–1968)

Austrian physicist Lise Meitner is famous for her experiment on 'transuranium-elements' with Fritz Strassmann and Otto Hahn. The experiment helped them discover the nuclear fission of uranium and thorium in 1938.

As momentous as this discovery was, Lise Meitner's achievements as a person go far beyond it. She suffered discrimination in her lifetime for being a woman. She grew up in an era when women were banned from public institutions of higher education. However, her determination and aptitude secured her positions that were rare for candidates of her gender to attain. German theoretical physicist and founder of the quantum theory Max Planck, who normally did not allow female students in his classroom, let her attend his lectures and appointed her his assistant within a year. She was also the first German woman to secure the post of full professor in physics.

Meitner started working with Otto Hahn on the 'transuranium research' program in 1935. Being a Jew, she was forced to leave Austria when the Nazis arrived in 1938. She moved to Stockholm and resumed her collaboration with Hahn through letters and secret meetings in Copenhagen. With her help, Hahn discovered the nuclear fission of heavy nuclei in the same year. Hahn could not credit her when he published their work due to the Nazi persecution of Jews and he was the sole recipient of the Nobel Prize in 1944. She never won the award, even though she was nominated for it more than ten times.

Albert Einstein rightly called Meitner the 'German Marie Curie.' After the Second World War ended, she received numerous accolades. In 1949 she was awarded the Max Planck Medal together with Hahn, for extraordinary achievement in theoretical physics. More recently, in 1997, Element 109 was named 'meitnerium' after her.

"You must not blame us scientists for the use to which war technicians have put our discoveries."

— Lise Meitner

Rachel Carson

(1907–1964)

Conservation of our natural environment is a burning issue for the world today. This was, however, not considered important up to the first half of the twentieth century. Industrial development, scientific advancement and high productivity were the main agendas for most governments. It took the efforts of one person to bring conservation to the limelight and that person was American marine biologist, environmentalist and writer, Rachel Carson.

Carson had a passion for both biology and nature writing. Her book *Silent Spring* focused on the harmful effects of pesticides, especially DDT, on the environment. Even before its publication, the book had garnered brickbats from the chemical industry. Velsicol Chemical Company threatened to sue the publishers and several articles promoting pesticide use were published as a pre-emptive measure. Many biochemists and chemical industrialists attacked her harshly, casting doubts on her credentials as she was a marine biologist, not a biochemist. One of her most vehement critics, American Cyanamid biochemist Robert White-Stevens said, "If man were to follow the teachings of Miss Carson, we would return to the Dark Ages." Fortunately for Carson, she had her fair share of backers from the academic community. Following a CBS Reports special program on television that featured interviews of both Carson and her critics, the general opinion of the American public swerved in her favor, prompting the President's Science Advisory Committee to launch a review of the dangers of pesticides. Its report supported the claims of Carson and the vilification campaign led by the chemical industry died down.

Carson died in 1964 but the impact of her work is still strongly felt and the ecological activism it initiated has never lost momentum. She was posthumously awarded the Presidential Medal of Freedom, the highest civilian honor in the United States, in 1980.

"*In nature nothing exists alone.*"

— Rachel Carson

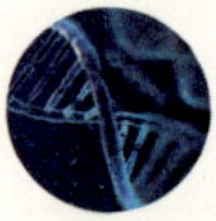

Rosalind Franklin

(1920–1958)

Rosalind Franklin was a winner from an early age, doing extremely well in both academics and sports. After graduating from Cambridge University at the age of twenty-one, she accepted a research position at the British Coal Utilization Research Association (BCURA) in 1942 and earned a PhD in 1945. Two years later she moved to Paris and became an expert X-ray crystallographer.

Such accomplishments were remarkable for a woman in the first half of the twentieth century, but Franklin did not stop there. Her research on coal, the polio and tobacco mosaic viruses and graphite were considered seminal in their respective fields. Her single greatest triumph, however, was her work on the structure of DNA. For this, she enjoyed recognition only after her death.

While Franklin's gender did not hamper her talent, it certainly prejudiced others from valuing her worth as a scientist. When she began working at King's College, London, in 1951, Maurice Wilkins, her colleague, would not accept her as an equal. Without taking her permission, Wilkins shared her crystallographic images of DNA with another male scientist, James Watson. The X-ray diffraction images of DNA developed by Franklin played a key role in the discovery of the DNA double helix. Watson and Francis Crick went on to publish their findings about the DNA structure in *Nature*, in which Franklin's work featured only as a supporting article.

In 1962, four years after Franklin's death from ovarian cancer, Watson, Wilkins and Crick together won the Nobel Prize in Physiology or Medicine for the double-helix model of DNA. But this time, both Watson and Crick acknowledged their debt to Franklin; Watson even stated that Franklin should have shared a Nobel Prize in Chemistry with Wilkins. In recent decades, several posthumous honors have been conferred upon Rosalind Franklin in recognition of her pioneering work.

"But science and everyday life cannot and should not be separated."

— Rosalind Franklin

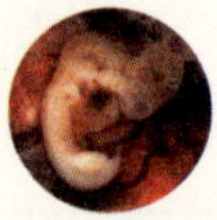

Subhash Mukhopadhyay

(1931–1981)

In 2003 the Indian Council for Medical Research (ICMR), along with Hope Infertility Clinic and Inter Academy Biomedical Science Forum, felicitated two people to mark the silver jubilee of IVF (in vitro fertilization) in India: Prof. Sunit Mukherjee and Kanupriya Aggarwal. Dr. Mukherjee had been a part of the IVF team to produce India's first and the world's second (just sixty-seven days after the first) test-tube baby. Kanupriya was the test-tube baby 'Durga.' The one person missing in the celebration was Dr. Subhash Mukhopadhyay, the scientist who made the miracle happen in 1978.

While Robert G. Edwards, the developer of IVF, was awarded the Nobel Prize in Physiology or Medicine in 2010, Dr. Mukhopadhyay was mocked by his peers and his findings were dismissed by the review committee appointed by the West Bengal government as 'bogus.' He was transferred to the ophthalmic department, preventing him from working with hormones, a key and unique feature of the procedure he had developed for fertilization. He was banned from participating in international conferences. Bureaucratic neglect and ostracism eventually led him to end his life in his Calcutta (Kolkata) residence in 1981. It was Dr. T. C. Anand Kumar, India's second scientist to produce a test-tube baby, who worked hard to bring credit to his predecessor. Following the publication of Dr. Kumar's investigation in 1997, Dr. Mukhopadhyay has been recognized in scientific circles for his achievements.

It has been estimated that almost 5 million babies have been born worldwide since 1978 with the help of IVF and other Assisted Reproductive Technology (ART). With the introduction of improved methods and reduced social stigma, more and more couples are openly seeking such treatments. Dr. Mukhopadhyay was unfortunately a victim of the conservative culture of his time. The innovations he brought to the field, such as cryopreservation of the embryos, continue to be used today.

"I am not a trophy but I am proud to be the living example of the work of a genius."

— **Durga** *on Dr. Subhash Mukhopadhyay*

ACKNOWLEDGEMENTS

PHOTO CREDITS

Cover	Kenny Tong/Shutterstock.com
Pages 2-3	Joseph Nicolas Robert-Fleury/Wikimedia Commons
Page 4	Andreas Cellarius/Space.com
Page 5	Wikimedia Commons
Page 6 (extreme left)	Andreas Cellarius/Space.com
Page 6 (middle left)	Wikimedia Commons
Page 6 (left)	Vitstudio/Shutterstock.com
Page 6 (center)	Supertrooper/Shutterstock.com
Page 6 (right)	The Birth Centenary Committee, printed by P.C. Ray/Wikimedia Commons
Page 6 (middle right)	Romolo Tavani/Shutterstock.com
Page 6 (extreme right)	Linda Bucklin/Shutterstock.com
Page 6-7 (bottom)	Wikimedia Commons
Page 14	Wikimedia Commons
Page 15	Gerardus Cremonensis/Wikimedia Commons
Page 22	Wikimedia Commons
Page 23 (foreground)	Andrea Bonaiuto/Wikimedia Commons
Page 23 (background)	Wikimedia Commons
Page 30	Andreas Cellarius/Space.com
Page 31	Jan Matejko/Wikimedia Commons
Page 38	NikiNomad/Shutterstock.com
Page 39 (foreground)	Liberowolf/NikoNomad/Shutterstock.com
Page 39 (background)	Wikimedia Commons
Page 46	Giuseppe Bertini/Wikimedia Commons
Page 47 (foreground)	Giuseppe Bertini/Wikimedia Commons
Page 47 (background)	Adriaen van de Venne/Wikimedia Commons
Page 54	Linda Bucklin/Shutterstock.com
Page 55 (foreground)	Leonard Darwin/Wikimedia Commons; Punch Magazine/Wikimedia Commons
Page 55 (background)	Petter Bockman/Wikimedia Commons
Page 62	Supertrooper/Shutterstock.com
Page 63 (foreground)	Supertrooper/Shutterstock.com; Wikimedia Commons
Page 63 (background)	Supertrooper/Shutterstock.com
Page 70	Roman Sigaev/Shutterstock.com
Page 71 (foreground)	Roman Sigaev/Shutterstock.com; Wikimedia Commons
Page 71 (background)	Roman Sigaev/Shutterstock.com

Page 78	The Birth Centenary Committee, printed by P.C. Ray/ Wikimedia Commons
Page 79 (foreground)	The Birth Centenary Committee, printed by P.C. Ray/ Wikimedia Commons; Xelena/Shutterstock.com
Page 79 (background)	SmallAtomWorks/Shutterstock.com
Page 86	Roman Sigaev/Shutterstock.com
Page 87 (foreground)	TTstudio/Shutterstock.com; Wikimedia Commons
Page 87 (background)	TTstudio/Shutterstock.com
Page 94	Romolo Tavani/Shutterstock.com
Page 95	U.S. Fish and Wildlife Service
Page 102	Vitstudio/Shutterstock.com
Page 103 (foreground)	Vitstudio/Shutterstock.com
Page 103 (background)	T. Moravec/Wikimedia Commons
Page 110	Ed Uthman/Wikimedia Commons
Page 111 (background)	Ekem/Wikimedia Commons
Endpaper	Joseph Nicolas Robert-Fleury/Wikimedia Commons

Beyond IMAGINATION

PERSECUTED FOR THEIR IDEAS

1.	Introduction	6
2.	Rhazes	14
3.	Averroes	22
4.	Nicolaus Copernicus	30
5.	Giordano Bruno	38
6.	Galileo Galilei	46
7.	Charles Darwin	54
8.	Gregor Mendel	62
9.	Ludwig Boltzmann	70
10.	Jagadish Chandra Bose	78
11.	Lise Meitner	86
12.	Rachel Carson	94
13.	Rosalind Franklin	102
14.	Subhash Mukhopadhyay	110